ACTIVITIES
for
COUNSELING
UNDERACHIEVERS

Jeanne Bleuer

Susanna Palomares

Garry Walz

cover design: Doug Armstrong Graphic Design
editor: Dianne Schilling

Published by Innerchoice Publishing
PO Box 1185
Torrance, CA 90505

ISBN 1-56499-016-8

ERIC/CASS
School of Education
University of North Carolina
Greensboro, NC 27412

This publication was prepared with partial funding from the Office of
Educational Research and Improvement, U.S. Department of Education. The
opinions expressed in this report do not necessarily reflect the positions or
policies of OERI, the Department of Education, or ERIC/CASS.

ACTIVITIES
for
COUNSELING
UNDERACHIEVERS

Contents

Introduction

Few areas of skill building are likely to pay as big dividends in improved grades and out of school rewards as improving your ability to achieve. Conventional wisdom would have it that the way to achieve more is to study harder —put in longer hours and avoid the distraction of other people. Research would suggest something different — study smarter, not necessarily harder, and use other students as a helpful support group. This book provides teachers, counselors, and students the tools they need to improve both their perceptions of themselves as achievers and their ability to apply effective learning strategies.

Key to the successful use of this book is the Achievement Potential Survey, an instrument for helping students determine what is right about their achievement and where they can make improvements. Following the survey is an extensive collection of relevant activities which the teacher or counselor can use to help students practice concrete behaviors that will enhance their ability and motivation to achieve.

If you are someone who likes to know the rationale behind activities and would like an informative analysis of research and experience on improving achievement, you will find the companion volume, *Counseling Underachievers*,* a very useful addition to your library of resources.

---

* Jeanne C. Bleuer, *Counseling Underachievers*. ERIC/CASS, UNCG, Greensboro, NC 27412, (800) 414-9769

How to Use This Book

To maximize the benefits of using the resources in this book, we recommend a systematic implementation over the period of a semester. Provide each student with some type of folder to be used as an "achievement portfolio" in which he/ she can collect such items as the results and analysis of his/her *Assessment Potential Survey*, action plans, notes from individual and group counseling or discussion sessions, and an "Achievement Insights" log.

For individual students or small groups, you may wish to select those activities that best address the specific problem areas of the students (as revealed by their *Assessment Potential Survey*). As an ongoing classroom or group counseling project, however, we recommend the use of as many of the different activities as possible. Even though the activities may represent issues that are not particularly problematic for some students, the sharing of insights and ideas with one another can be very beneficial for the entire group.

The Achievement Potential Survey is written with directions to the student. Older students should be able to complete and self score the survey. However, if you are working with younger children, you may need to provide more directions in taking the survey and work closely with them on the scoring. You may need to explain in terms that are on their levels the information provided in each item measured.

It is recommended that the teacher or counselor work individually with *all* students to discuss and problem solve the findings of the Achievement Potential Summary Sheet and Follow-up Survey Summary Sheet. This is also the time to acknowledge and encourage areas of strength, growth, and positive direction in the students.

The group activities should be approached with the same attitude. Be prepared to gear the activities and language up or down depending on the experience, age, and ethnicity of your students.

If you administer the survey at the beginning of the semester and work with the students and involve them in the activities, you will find it valuable to administer the Achievement Potential Follow-up Survey (Page 115) at the end of the semester. Helping the students to see their growth and development as reflected in the follow-up survey will be a powerful step toward enhancing achievement.

Achievement Potential Survey

For each of the following sets of statements, mark the one that best describes you.

1. My Academic Ability

___ A. In terms of basic ability, I could get straight A's if I really wanted to.
___ B. I really don't have what it takes to get good grades in school.
___ C. A lot of kids are smarter than I am, but I could get better grades if I just worked harder.

2. Knowledge I Already Have

___ A. I think I have a pretty good background to take on the assignments my teachers make.
___ B. I have a hard time understanding what's going on in school because there's a lot I should have learned before I got to these classes.
___ C. Sometimes I feel I don't know as much as I should to be able to do the work my teachers expect.

3. My Past Learning Experiences

___ A. Doing well in school has always been easy for me.
___ B. School work has always been hard for me.
___ C. My successes and failures in school are pretty well balanced; sometimes I've done pretty well, but other times I've had some problems understanding the work.

4. My Study Skills

___ A. I have some pretty good strategies for tackling assignments and getting my school work done.
___ B. Even when I try to study, it doesn't seem to help.
___ C. My study skills are OK, but they could be improved.

5. My Learning Style

___ A. I know exactly how I can arrange my study sessions so that I can do my best work.
___ B. I've never really thought much about how I work best.
___ C. I know a little bit about my learning style, but haven't really figured out what's best.

6. My Ability to See Connections

___ A. I can almost always make a connection between an idea or concept in my studies and my own personal life.
___ B. Most of the ideas or concepts presented in my studies seem abstract, and seldom can I see any connection to my own life.
___ C. Sometimes I see connections between what I'm studying and my own personal situation, but not very often.

7. My General Mood

___ A. In general, I feel pretty positive and don't have a lot of trouble with bad moods interfering with my school work.
___ B. There are a lot of things bothering me right now and they keep me from concentrating on school work.
___ C. Sometimes I have trouble concentrating on school work because I just don't feel very good about myself and my life.

8. My Health

____ A. I'm in good health and hardly ever miss school because of illness.
____ B. I've missed a lot of school because of illness.
____ C. I've missed some school because of illness; even when I am in school I often don't do as well as I could because I don't feel very well.

9. My Feelings About Achievement

____ A. Doing well in school is really important to me.
____ B. Sometimes I feel like not doing well in school just to make my parents mad.
____ C. Doing well in school seems to be more important to others (my parents, teachers, etc.) than it is to me.

10. My Personal Life/Career Goals

____ A. I want to go to college or get a good job when I finish school.
____ B. I haven't really given much thought to what I want to do when I finish school.
____ C. I've been thinking about it, but I'm not sure what I want to do when I finish school.

11. My Desire to Impress Others

____ A. There is at least one particular person in my life that I want to impress with my school achievement.
____ B. I really don't care much what anyone else thinks about my school achievement as long as they don't give me a hard time about it.
____ C. I like it when others are impressed with my school work, but there's no one in particular that I want to impress.

12. My Willingness to Risk Failure

___ A. I usually volunteer answers to questions my teachers ask even if I'm afraid my answers might be wrong.

___ B. I only answer questions and turn in assignments if I know I'm right and my work is well done.

___ C. Sometimes I'm afraid to answer questions in class because it would be too embarrassing if I was wrong.

13. My Willingness to Tackle Unpleasant Tasks

___ A. Whenever I have a tough assignment, I try to get started on it as soon as possible.

___ B. I always put off tough assignments until the very last minute and often don't leave myself enough time to finish them.

___ C. I often put off tough assignments as long as possible, but usually manage to get them done.

14. My Willingness to Stick With a Problem Until It's Solved

___ A. I'm the kind of person who likes to stick with a problem until it's solved, no matter how long it takes.

___ B. If I can't solve a problem right away, I get pretty impatient and will usually give up.

___ C. I try to give a reasonable amount of time and effort to solving a problem; but if it takes too long, I quit.

15. The Amount of Time I Spend on Homework

___ A. I usually spend at least 10 hours a week on homework.

___ B. I usually spend less than 5 hours a week on homework.

___ C. I usually spend between 5 and 10 hours a week on homework.

16. My Family's Expectations

___ A. My family expects me to do well in school.
___ B. My family doesn't really care how well I do in school.
___ C. My family is kind of interested in how well I do in school.

17. My Family's Support

___ A. My parents do everything they can to provide the help and resources I need to do my school work.
___ B. It's hard for me to get my school work done at home because I often have to do things for my family like taking care of younger brothers and sisters, working a part-time job, helping out in the house, etc.
___ C. My family is pretty good about giving me time to study, but it's pretty much up to me to make sure I get it all done.

18. My Friends' Achievement and Expectations

___ A. Most of my friends get pretty good grades and think I should too.
___ B. Most of my friends don't do very well in school and would be very surprised if I was able to do well.
___ C. Most of my friends get about average grades and expect about the same from me.

19. My Friends' Support

___ A. Most of my friends are willing to help me do well in school.
___ B. Most of my friends don't really care how I do in school and resent it if I decide to study rather than spend time relaxing with them.
___ C. Sometimes my friends can be helpful to me; other times not.

20. The Difficulty of My School Work

___ A. The work expected in most of my classes is not very difficult.

___ B. The work expected in most of my classes is very difficult.

___ C. The work expected in most of my classes is somewhat difficult.

21. The Nature of My Assignments

___ A. In general, my school assignments are pretty interesting, and it seems like what I'm learning is important.

___ B. Most of my school work is pretty boring and has nothing to do with real life.

___ C. Sometimes my assignments are interesting, but usually they're just something to get done.

22. My Teachers' Expectations

___ A. My teachers all think I'm capable of doing very good work.

___ B. Most of my teachers don't expect me to be able to do very good work.

___ C. Some of my teachers think I'm capable of doing good work; others just expect me to do average work.

23. My Teachers' Support

___ A. My teachers are very good about providing whatever help I need to complete my assignments.

___ B. In general, my teachers seem to feel that getting the work done is my problem, not theirs.

___ C. My teachers are fairly good about providing help.

24. My School's Resources

___ A. My school has a lot of good resources (library, counselors, study halls, etc.) to help students with their school work.

___ B. My school doesn't really have very many resources.

___ C. My school is OK in terms of resources.

25. My School's "Climate"

___ A. My school is a very good one; I enjoy being there.

___ B. My school is pretty bad; I hate being there.

___ C. My school is OK; sometimes it's good to be there, other times it's not.

26. My Participation in Extracurricular Activities

___ A. I am very active in my school's extracurricular activities.

___ B. I am not at all active in my school's extracurricular activities.

___ C. I take part in a few of my school's extracurricular activities.

Achievement Potential

Summary Sheet

Part I. <u>Can</u> I do well in school?

	Asset	Barrier	Concern
1. Academic Ability			
2. Current Knowledge			
3. Past Experiences			
4. Study Skills			
5. Learning Style			
6. Seeing Connections			

Part II. Do I really <u>want</u> to do well in school?

	Asset	Barrier	Concern
7. General Mood			
8. Health			
9. Feelings About Achievement			
10. Life/Career Goals			
11. Impressing Others			
12. Risking Failure			
13. Tackling Unpleasant Tasks			
14. Sticking With a Problem			
15. Time Spent on Homework			

Part III. What effect have my family and friends had on my achievement?

	Asset	Barrier	Concern
16. Family's Expectations			
17. Family's Support			
18. Friends' Expectations			
19. Friends' Support			

Part IV. How "inviting" is my school?

	Asset	Barrier	Concern
20. Difficulty of School Work			
21. Nature of Assignments			
22. Teachers' Expectations			
23. Teachers' Support			
24. School Resources			
25. School Climate			
26. Extracurricular Activities			

Scoring and Interpreting Your Achievement Potential

Sorting Out Your ABCs

Each of the items on the *Achievement Potential Survey* represents a potential *Asset* - a strength you can use to improve your achievement; a *Barrier* - an obstacle that can interfere with your achievement; or a *Concern* - an area that could go either way.

As we review each item, place an X in the appropriate column on your *Achievement Potential Summary Sheet*. If you checked sentence A, put an X under Asset. If you checked sentence B, put an X under Barrier. If you checked sentence C, put an X under Concern. For some items, the concept may be easier to understand after you read the explanation. If, after careful thought, you feel that your original response doesn't really reflect your own situation, feel free to change your response so that the item is accurately categorized as an asset, barrier, or concern.

Part I.

The six items in Part I of the *Achievement Potential Survey* deal with how confident you are that you *can* do well in school.

1. Academic Ability

How you see yourself in terms of your academic ability is probably the most important factor in determining how much effort you put into your school work. If you feel that you're just not smart enough to do the work, then most likely you won't even try. On the other hand, if you're confident that you can do it if you really want to, then you can count this as one of your major assets and move on to looking at other factors that may be keeping you from working up to your full potential.

2. Current Knowledge

Learning always builds on knowledge you already have. You can't learn to spell until you know the letters of the alphabet. You have to know basic math before you can learn algebra or accounting. Sometimes you can reach a certain grade level or enroll in certain courses without having learned everything you need to know to understand the new concepts that are presented. When you find yourself in this situation, it's easy to panic and begin to doubt your ability. Being able to recognize this situation and get help to "back up and fill the gaps" can restore your confidence in yourself and help you move on to higher levels of achievement.

3. Past Experiences

The experiences you have had in the past play a major role in determining what you expect in the future. If learning has always been easy for you, then you will be confident that it will continue to be so. On the other hand, if your past efforts at learning have not always been successful, you are not likely to expect much of yourself in future learning experiences and may decide "why try?" when, with just a little more effort, you could be replacing your collection of failures with a collection of successes.

4. Study Skills

Knowing how to study effectively can make a big difference in whether learning seems to come easy or hard. "Average" students who have developed good techniques for taking notes, preparing for tests, etc., can often outperform "bright" ones who approach studying in a haphazard manner. There are many good handbooks available that can provide you with tips and strategies that have proved to be effective for students of all ages. If this is one of your barriers, ask your teacher, counselor, or librarian to help you find one of these books.

5. Learning Style

Unlike study skills that are somewhat standardized for everyone, learning style refers to what works for you personally. Do you work better alone or with others? In a quiet room or with your stereo turned up loud with your favorite music? By reading printed material, listening to a lecture, or seeing a demonstration? Early in the morning, right after school, or late at night? Understanding your own best learning style and setting up your study plan to capitalize on what works best for you can greatly improve your achievement.

6. Seeing Connections

Having an "Ah-hah!" experience where something suddenly clicks and you can see an important connection between what you are studying and things that are happening in your own life can be a real boost to your perception of your mental abilities. Fortunately, you don't have to wait for such an experience to happen. Through practice in looking for such connections, you can actually increase the number of times you find them.

Part II.

The nine items in Part II of the *Achievement Potential Survey* deal with personal values, goals, and characteristics that help to determine how much you *want* to reach a high level of school achievement.

7. General Mood

Your mood, of course, can change from one day to the next and even from one hour to the next. However, if you are generally a fairly positive and optimistic person, you're much more likely to feel like taking on the challenges of school work than if you are more pessimistic and negative.

8. Health

If you're not feeling well, it's very hard to concentrate on what's going on in class, to do well on tests, and to complete your assignments. And missing school can make matters even worse because once you get behind it's hard to catch up.

9. Feelings About Achievement

Obviously, if achieving is important to you *personally*, you are going to want to do everything you can to make it happen. On the other hand, if you're just trying to satisfy the demands of others (parents, teachers, etc.), you *might pretend* to put in the effort, but you really won't do as well as you could.

10. Life/Career Goals

In the previous item, doing well in school is seen as an end in itself and the rewards you get in the form of praise and recognition are immediate. In this item the rewards you expect are more long-term — getting into a good college, getting a good job, etc. In general, the more specific you can be about what you want to do when you graduate (even if you change your mind several times), the more relationship you can see between the importance of what you are doing now and the achievement of your life/career goals.

11. Impressing Others

In a previous item, we made the point that just trying to satisfy the demands of others is not particularly effective in improving achievement. However, having a special person in your life (parent, older brother or sister, teacher, counselor, friend, coach, etc.) who is very important to you and someone you *want* to impress can be very helpful in seeing you through the tough times on your road to academic achievement.

12. Risking Failure

Continually striving for a high level of achievement means taking the risk that sometimes you will fall short of your goal. Sometimes your answers will be wrong; sometimes your papers won't be perfect. Developing the courage to risk the embarrassment of being wrong can greatly increase your active participation in classroom activities and your willingness to turn in work that is the best you can do even if it isn't perfect.

13. Tackling Unpleasant Tasks

Procrastination! It's probably the toughest problem students face. It's so much easier to do what's fun now and worry about school work later. It's also kind of scary to start on something you're not sure you can finish even to your own level of satisfaction, let alone what you think your teacher expects.

14. Sticking With a Problem

Even with the best study skills, learning new concepts and solving complex problems can be very frustrating and can take more time than you expect. Being able to see these situations as challenges to be met and having a strong desire to hang in there until you figure it out is an asset that will pay huge dividends both in your school work and in your other life situations.

15. Time Spent on Homework

The research is clear that the more time you spend "on task" the greater your learning will be. Good study skills can increase your effectiveness and efficiency and reduce your stress, but you still need to plan on spending a fair amount of time each week on homework if you want to assure a high level of learning and achievement.

Part III.

Parts I and II dealt with "internal" factors, your own personal thoughts, feelings, values, and personality traits. Parts III and IV deal with "external" factors — friends, family, your school, your school work, etc. To a certain extent, these factors are "fixed" and you may or may not be able to change them. What you can change, however, is how you interpret and respond to them. The four items in Part III deal with the impact that your family and friends have both on your confidence that you can achieve and your desire to achieve.

These items may have been difficult to answer because it's hard to put all of your family members in one category and all of your friends in one category. One parent may be very supportive while another or a brother or sister is not. Some of your friends may be high achievers and others not. At this time, just give your best estimate in terms of their overall impact on your achievement. However, in your more in-depth review of your assets and barriers, either alone or with a teacher or counselor, you should look at each important person in your life as an individual and try to determine how that person helps or hinders your achievement.

16. Family's Expectations

If your family expects you to do well in school, they must have confidence that you have the ability to do well. Again, that makes it easier for you to have confidence in yourself. However, if your family doesn't seem to care how well you do in school, that doesn't necessarily mean they doubt your ability. It could mean that other things are more important to them than education. In either case, feeling that your family has confidence in your ability is helpful, but how you perceive your ability is more important.

17. Family's Support

If your family is the type that goes the extra mile to provide the help and resources you need to do well in school, consider yourself very fortunate. Even if they seem to be too involved at times, that's an easier problem to deal with than families that make it difficult or even impossible for their children to study at home or to attend school regularly.

18. Friends' Expectations

Kids tend to associate with other kids who are achieving at about the same level. If your friends don't expect you to get good grades, you probably don't expect much of yourself. If, however, your friends place a high value on achievement, it's very likely that you want to achieve at least at the level that they do.

19. Friends' Support

Good friends not only expect you to do well, but will also do what they can to be helpful whether it's helping you work through a tough assignment or just agreeing not to interfere with time you've set aside to study.

Part IV.

These last six items deal with factors related to your school and school work. In other words, how "inviting" is your school? Is it a place where you feel you can and want to achieve? As discussed above regarding family and friends, it may be difficult to answer the items regarding your teachers. Again, at this time, try to think of the overall effect your teachers have had on you and look at the effect that specific teachers have had on you later when you do a more in-depth analysis of factors affecting your achievement.

20. Difficulty of School Work

If your school work seems "do-able," you will be confident that you can do what is expected by just putting forth the necessary effort. On the other hand, if it seems too difficult, you will most likely lose confidence in yourself and will decide not to put any effort into participating in class or completing assignments.

21. Nature of Assignments

If your assignments are challenging, interesting, and meaningful to you, you will most likely enjoy doing them and will want to do them well. If they aren't, doing them will seem like a drag and a waste of time.

22. Teachers' Expectations

If your teachers have confidence in you, it's easier for you to have confidence in yourself. If your teachers don't expect much from you, you probably won't expect much from yourself.

23. Teachers' Support

Teachers that are encouraging and helpful make it easier for students to *want* to actively participate and do well.

24. School Resources

Most schools have the resources that students need to accomplish their learning tasks; but students aren't always aware of these resources and often don't take advantage of them.

25. School Climate

In these days, schools are not always the safe havens they used to be. Even when there is little physical danger to students, a cold or hostile psychological environment can make it very difficult for students to relax and focus on learning.

26. Extracurricular Activities

In general, students who participate actively in extracurricular activities see school as a fun, interesting, and comfortable place to be. Usually, this desire to be active and involved transfers to the classroom as well. But, not always. Sometimes these students get so involved in their extracurricular activities that they don't have time to do their homework, prepare for tests, etc. For this item, place your X in the column that best reflects the impact that your involvement in extracurricular activities has on your school work, regardless of how you responded to the item.

Analyzing and Interpreting Your Achievement Potential Summary Sheet

Now that you have classified all 26 factors into assets, barriers, and concerns, take a look at your Achievement Potential Summary Sheet and see if you can identify any patterns.

Some of the patterns you could look for are:

1. Which column has the most X's — Assets, Barriers, or Concerns? What conclusions can you draw from this?

2. Add up all the X's you have under Assets in Parts I and II. This represents the number of strengths you feel you have going for you within yourself. How does this compare with the number of X's you have under Barriers in Parts I and II? In other words, when it comes to improving achievement, are you your own best friend or your own worst enemy?

3. How does your pattern of Assets and Barriers for Parts I and II compare with your pattern for Parts III and IV? Do you have more assets within yourself or outside yourself? Do you have more barriers within yourself or outside yourself? What can you do to capitalize on your "outside" assets? What can you do to reduce the impact of some of your "outside" barriers?

4. Look at each X in the Concern column. If you had to make a prediction based on your current life situation, which ones are likely to become Assets and which ones are likely to become Barriers? What could you do to increase the odds of them becoming Assets?

Developing an Action Plan

Based on your own analysis of your Achievement Potential Summary Sheet and your discussions of your Summary Sheet with other students and your teacher or counselor, identify the five most critical factors currently affecting your achievement.

For each of these five factors:

1. Identify what you see as the major problem.

2. What you want to change.

3. List the steps you need to take starting NOW to achieve this change.

What Would You Do?

Simulated Problem Case Histories for Student Discussion

Introduction

The following case histories are actual situations
which have been experienced by students. Unlike
some textbook problems, there are no easy or quick
solutions to them. They do, however, provide an
opportunity for students to analyze the factors
affecting achievement that have been presented.
They offer a way for you to help students get on
top of the challenges facing them — rather than
struggling to get out from under them. They can
also help students to develop proactive responses
for resolving difficult situations before they become
perpetual problems.

Student Outcomes

Through the use of the case histories, students will:

- Learn how to identify the specific factors that affect a particular student's achievement.
- Understand how interacting with peers in analyzing achievement challenges can improve insight into the situation and increase the quality of the recommended responses or solutions to the problem.
- Gain skill in customizing an achievement strategy that fits an individual student's personality and situation.

Procedure

Form students into groups of four to six each. Explain that the purpose of the activity is for them to gain practice in applying what they've learned about analyzing achievement factors to actual situations experienced by students. This, in turn will help them better analyze their own achievement challenges.

Present each student with a copy of the first case history (Challenge #1). Have one person in each group read the case history to the other group members while they read along on their own copy. Then have each person independently write down his/her analysis of the important factors present, what achievement concepts apply, and the actions he/she would recommend. Each person should then be given 3-5 minutes to present his/her ideas to the group. The group should then discuss the situation and reach a consensus that incorporates the best ideas from each person's analysis.

The group should end with a brief discussion of what each participant learned from the activity and how it could apply to his or her own situation. Have participants keep a personal log of "Achievement Insights" which describes ideas they have acquired about their own situational challenges as a result of analyzing the case histories.

In subsequent sessions, repeat the process for Challenges 2 through 4.

Challenge #1 "Stop Giving Me Excuses and Get to Work!"

After reviewing his school achievement situation, John decided his ability was OK, but he lacked an organized way of going about studying. Taking into account his own learning style, home situation, and the nature of his homework, John put together the best elements of his own learning style which combined individual and group studying. He decided that he could overcome his cramped and hectic home situation by forming a study group of compatible friends who scheduled regular times to meet. This strategy also carried out the teacher's suggestion to work as a team on the problems she presented.

The problem, however, was that John's parents thought he was procrastinating by not studying when they wanted him to — immediately after school and after dinner. They saw his "study team" as a weak excuse to hang out with his friends and avoid studying. The situation has become increasingly tense and his parents are now forbidding him to go out until he shows them what he has finished by himself. John has become very angry, accusing his parents of trying to run his life and not giving him any credit for being able to solve his own problems.

What are some of John's achievement assets and barriers?

What is likely to happen if John doesn't take positive action to improve the situation?

What should he do?

Challenge #2 "Getting Good Grades Doesn't Mean Very Much"

If you were to wander into Millford High School and ask students to identify someone who really seemed to "have it together," probably the majority of them would say Mary Winter. Attractive, popular, and active in school and community organizations, May impressed everyone as a person with a bright future. Everyone, that is, except Mary herself, her counselor, and some of her teachers. They knew that she was doing only fair work in her classes and that, with her academic record, admission to the college she wanted to attend was doubtful. Mary kept it to herself, but she was puzzled and more than a little worried about how she could be sailing right along on most things but struggling with her pre-college track classes. Each semester her academic record got a little bit worse, so she tried to compensate for it by doing even better in her non-academic activities. "After all," Mary said to herself, "grades aren't everything. I've known a lot of kids with good grades who didn't amount to anything."

What are some of Mary's assets and barriers in terms of improving her academic achievement?

What are some of the possible reasons for Mary's problems in her classes?

Is she right in downplaying the importance of school grades?

What does Mary probably think of her academic ability?

What steps should Mary take to improve her situation?

Challenge #3 "An Honor Student in the Eyes of Others"

At the top of his class academically, Wong Su had an enviable academic record — or so it seemed. To himself, however, Wong was anything but a winner, One of four children from strict parents (recent immigrants from Korea), Wong lived in fear of not being at the top of everything he did. He selected classes (and cancelled them) based on how well his investigation told him he could do. He chose his homework topics very carefully and flattered the smartest students so they would share their homework with him.

In discussions with his counselor, Wong said his greatest goal in life was to be an "outstanding success and never fail at anything." He would go without sleep to try to make an assignment perfect, but would quickly feign illness or give elaborate excuses to get out of something if he wasn't doing well at it. When anyone asked Wong what he wanted to do when he graduated from high school, he would smile and, with more assurance than he felt, tell them, "I want to get into the very best university and become very successful, which would make may parents very proud."

What are some of Wong's assets and barriers in terms of academic achievement?

Are his goals appropriate for him?

Is Wong's schooling likely to get easier or harder over time?

What actions should Wong take to improve his situation?

Challenge #4 "A Beautiful Building, But . . . "

Eisenhower High School is an unusually attractive example of contemporary school architecture. Persons seeing it for the first time frequently comment on how much they like it. Its attractive appearance, however, makes it all the more difficult for Kathy's parents to understand why she hates going to school. Though the reasons are not clear to her parents, they know that Kathy strongly feels that school is definitely not a place she wants to be.

An able student with many talents, Kathy has shown little interest in doing anything more than just getting by in school and has shunned involvement in anything "not required of me." The school administration and faculty have prided themselves in providing a college-like climate and treating students like adults. However, Kathy has experienced it as a lack of caring by teachers who are "too stuck up to sit down and talk with you." According to Kathy, "They just dump homework on you like you're some kind of computer."

When she was in elementary and junior high school, Kathy was a very warm and outgoing person. She liked her teachers, did well in her classes, and was very active in school activities. Now, however, she has become withdrawn socially and spends most of her time with a few close friends. Unlike her previous circle of friends who were good students and active in school activities, these new friends often skip school to hang out with an older crowd of high school dropouts.

What is likely happen if Kathy continues her present behavior?

What could her parents do?

What are her assets and barriers if she decides she wants to improve her school performance?

Student Activities

Progressive Relaxation

Objectives:

The students will:

— recognize the difference between tension and relaxation.
— understand and employ a process for relaxation.

Directions:

Even teens and young people may have chronically tense muscles. By tensing and relaxing muscle groups, one group at a time, they can identify specific muscles and recognize the difference between tension and relaxation. Deep muscle relaxation reduces physiological tension, and is incompatible with anxiety. Encourage the students to use this and other relaxation strategies prior to tests or other stress-producing activities, and they will be more likely to have a successful, positive experience.

You can lead your students in a progressive relaxation exercise by reading the directions on page 42.

Have the students either lie down or sit in a chair. In a pleasant voice, read aloud the directions on the sheet.

As students systematically tense and relax each muscle group, suggest that they use positive self-talk to assist in melting the tension. Messages like, "Relax, let all the tension dissolve," or "I am feeling calm and relaxed," will facilitate the relaxation process. You may want to distribute copies of the progressive relaxation exercise to those students who would like to have it for their personal use.

Do this activity on more than one occasion. It's a good way to begin any session, and is especially effective if the students come to class upset, agitated, or worried.

Progressive Relaxation

1. Sit straight in a comfortable chair and relax. Place your hands in your lap and your feet on the floor. Close your eyes.

2. Tense, tighten, or squeeze the muscles in your right hand into a fist and hold tightly for 5 seconds. Release, noticing the tension in your fist, hand, and forearm. Relax for 20 to 30 seconds. Repeat with your right hand, noticing the contrast between feelings of tension and relaxation. Repeat with your left hand and then make fists with both hands at the same time. (Remember to tighten for 5 seconds and release for 20 to 30 seconds each time.)

3. Bend your elbows and tense your biceps. Relax. Straighten your arms, feeling the difference between the tension and relaxation.

4. Wrinkle your forehead tightly. Smooth it out and relax. Frown and feel the strain throughout your forehead. Relax and let your forehead become smooth again.

5. Tightly squeeze your eyes closed. Relax. Keep them closed gently.

6. Clench your jaw, bite hard. Relax.

7. Press your head back as far as possible and notice the tension in your neck. Roll your head to the right and then to the left. Straighten your head and bring it forward.

8. Place your chin on your chest. Feel the tension in your throat. Relax. Bring your head to a comfortable position again. Lift your shoulders high in a shrug. Hold. Relax.

9. Breathe in and take a complete natural breath. Hold and notice the tension. Exhale. Repeat several times. Tighten your stomach and hold. Relax. Place your hand on your stomach. Breathe deeply, pushing your hand up. Hold and relax. Arch your back, being careful not to strain it. Relax the rest of your body.

10. Tighten your buttocks and thighs. Flex your thighs by pressing down with your heels as hard as you can. Relax. Curl your toes downward, making your calves tense. Relax. Bend your toes upward, feeling the tension in your shins. Relax.

11. Feel the heaviness in your lower body. Relax your feet, ankles, calves, shins, knees, thighs, and buttocks.

12. Relax shoulders, arms, hands, neck, jaw, and facial muscles.

Things I Find Useful

(Personal notes and ideas that make this activity work better for me)

Understanding Rules

Objectives:

The students will:

— demonstrate understanding of the need for school and classroom rules.
— describe how they benefit from school rules.
— develop rules for a simple game.

Materials:

a number of small, everyday items such as paper, markers, string, paper clips, poker chips, buttons, marbles, balls, jacks, etc.

Directions:

All schools and most classrooms have specific sets of rules that must be adhered to by all students. Students usually have little or no input into the establishment of such rules and, consequently, limited commitment to following them. We can, however, help students develop a better understanding of the purpose of rules, and how those rules may actually benefit them. Once they possess this understanding, students are more likely to cooperate in following rules, and their cooperation will in turn contribute to a more successful school experience.

As a prelude to a discussion about rules, involve the students in creating a game that includes the establishment of rules.

To stimulate creativity, start by selecting one item from the materials collection (a paper clip, for example), and ask the students to help you brainstorm 30 uses for that item. Announce a 4-minute time limit. Encourage imaginative and outrageous suggestions. Emphasize that when the class is brainstorming and being creative, *all* suggestions are accepted; *no* judgments or put-downs are allowed.

After the initial brainstorming session, divide the students into groups of six. Explain that each group is to create a simple game using any number of items from the collection that you have provided. Explain that the games may involve any number of players in any age group, but that every game must have a clear objective and established rules for play. Remind the students to be creative; however, warn them that they have only 15 minutes — not nearly enough time to create a game as involved as Monopoly.

Call time and ask for a synopsis of each game. If time permits, have each group briefly demonstrate its game

At the conclusion of the presentations, ask these and other questions, encouraging the students to discuss the need and value of rules.

Discussion Questions:

1. How important were the rules you came up with for your game?
2. In what other areas of our lives do we encounter rules?
3. Why do we have rules for things like sports, work, school, home?
4. How would football be different without rules? How would school be different?

Ask the following series of questions in relation to a series of specific school rules. Examine one rule at a time:

5. What are some specific benefits of this school rule? What are its limitations?
6. How could this rule be improved?
7. What are some ways in which this rule benefits you as an individual?
8. What would our school be like if this rule didn't exist?

Things I Find Useful

(Personal notes and ideas that make this activity work better for me)

Getting In at Our School

Objectives:

The students will:

— identify on- and off-campus organizations and extra-curricular activities.

— demonstrate strategies for building positive peer support systems.

Materials:

5-inch by 8-inch file cards

Directions:

Begin this activity by talking with the students about the importance of peer support. Ask them if they are aware of the fact that each time they make a friend, join an organization, help another student, or participate in a group activity, they are building a peer support group—a network of people they can turn to for:

— companionship and sharing,
— help with projects and problems,
— backing in reaching goals or making changes,
— cooperation when a group effort is required,
— protection if they're threatened or coerced,
— creativity when new ideas are called for.

Suggest that one of the best ways to strengthen and enlarge one's peer support group is to become involved in extra-curricular activities and on- and off-campus organizations. Point out that joining lots of organizations is not necessarily the objective—that simply becoming informed about an organization and making contact with one or two of its leaders can bring the entire organization within one's own network of resources.

Divide the students into groups of 3 to 5, and ask half of the groups to develop a list of on-campus organizations and the other half of the groups to develop a list of off-campus organizations (or volunteer opportunities) suitable for their age group. Brainstorm with the students methods that they can use to conduct their research. Give them until the next meeting to complete the assignment.

At the next meeting, put a list of all organizations researched by the students on the board. Ask each group to sign up to investigate one of them. Suggest that the students attend a meeting and/or talk to a leader in the organization and provide the following information on a 5-inch by 8-inch index card:

1. Name of the organization
2. Affiliated inside or outside of school
3. Purpose of the organization
4. Types of activities, and location and frequency of meetings
5. Qualifications to join
6. Procedure to join
7. Name of contact person or sponsor and room/phone number
8. Time and place of next meeting

Ask the groups to report their findings to the class. Post the index cards on a bulletin board or organize them in a file box so that the students will have easy access to the information gathered.

Encourage a discussion about what the students have learned, and how joining an organization can be helpful to them.

Things I Find Useful

(Personal notes and ideas that make this activity work better for me)

Sequencing Anger

Objectives:

The students will:

— demonstrate an understanding of an anger sequence: event-thoughts-feelings.
— practice substituting moderate thoughts for angry thoughts as one way of reducing anger.

Materials:

chalkboard and chalk, writing paper, pencils

Directions:

Tell the students that, in this activity, they will have an opportunity to discover a new way of handling anger. Ask them to consider that angry feelings are not actually caused by situations and events, but rather by the *thoughts* one has about those situations and events. When these thoughts about an event (often extreme) are identified, they can be replaced with different thoughts (usually more moderate) as one way of controlling anger. Explain to the students that you are going to demonstrate this concept using a chart on the board.

Write four headings across the top of the board: **Event, Thoughts, Feelings,** and **Substitute Thoughts.** Under the **Event** column, write *Mom won't let me go to the dance with my friends.* Skip the second column and ask the students what their feelings might be in this situation. The students will probably suggest words such as *mad, furious,* and *miserable.* Write several of these words in the **Feelings** column. Then go back to the **Thoughts** column, and ask the students what their thoughts might be concerning the same situation. Elicit answers such as these: *She's being mean. She doesn't understand how important it is to me. She never wants me to have fun.*

Explain to the students that it is not the event, but the *thoughts* about the event that cause the feelings. Refer to the sentences in the second column and point out that any of these thoughts about the event could create angry feelings. Explain that no situation, event, or person *makes* us have a particular feeling. Through our thoughts, we *choose* our feelings, even if we are not aware of it.

Next, suggest that if the thoughts recorded in the second column can be moderated, the feelings too will change. Help the students create new thought statements such as: *Mom thinks she is looking out for my safely. She has family plans the night of the dance and wants me to be with the family. There will be more dances this year.* Record them in the last column, **Substitute Thoughts**. Point out that these moderated thoughts will reduce the anger.

Distribute writing paper and pencils. Ask the students to divide their paper in half lengthwise creating two columns. Have them write the heading *Event* at the top of the left-hand column and the heading *Thoughts* at the top of the right-hand column. Next, instruct the students to turn their paper over and create two more columns. Direct them to write the headings *Feelings* and *Substitute Thoughts* above the left and right columns on this side.

Under the first heading, ask the students to list three real or hypothetical situations/events in which they are certain they would feel angry. In the second column (adjacent to each description), have them write the thoughts they would have in each situation. On the other side of the paper, ask them to write down the feelings that these thoughts would create. Finally, challenge the students to come up with moderated thoughts that could be substituted for the original thoughts about the situation.

When all of the students have completed their charts, invite individuals to share one or more of their "anger sequences." After each example, ask the group how their feelings might change as a result of the substitute thoughts. Emphasize that when they find themselves reacting to a situation too strongly, the students can improve their disposition by rethinking the situation. This ability takes practice and perseverance, but it works!

Discussion Questions:

To summarize, ask the students to think about and/or respond to the following questions:

—*Why do we choose to feel angry in certain situations?*
— *When you are angry, why is it important to rethink the situation?*
—*What is easy about sequencing anger? What is difficult about it?*

Things I Find Useful

(Personal notes and ideas that make this activity work better for me)

Wanted: Leadership

Objectives:

The students will identify individuals and systems able to provide assistance with specific school-related problems.

Materials:

one copy for each student of pages 57 and 58, "Leadership Styles"

Directions:

Begin by engaging the students in a discussion about leadership. Define leadership as:

...the act of influencing one or more people to move in the direction of a goal.

Point out that, depending on the situation, a variety of behaviors and characteristics define a leader. In one way or another, all leaders are able to identify goals and stimulate action that leads to the attainment of those goals. If they couldn't do that, they would not be leading—there would be nowhere to go. In your own words, say to the students: *How leaders lead varies from one person to another, and from one situation to another. Most leaders probably communicate well, at least orally. Some are good at developing teamwork. Others may demonstrate empathy, enthusiasm, self-confidence, decisiveness, perspective, style, humility, or a sense of humor. A few leaders may have all of these qualities. In some situations, a leader must be a good detective who searches out answers and better ways of doing things. In other situations, the leader's challenge is to motivate someone else to do the detective work. To be the leader in any situation, a person must recognize and respond to the needs of the followers in that situation. For example, if students need to talk to someone about career plans, but the logical person to see—their counselor—isn't familiar with very many fields and doesn't refer the students to other information sources, they will find other leaders. They will talk to teachers, librarians, friends, relatives, and business people. If a supervisor assigns a totally unfamiliar task to a worker but doesn't give the worker any ideas about how to accomplish the task, the worker will either identify other sources of leadership—coworkers, for example—or will learn the task entirely by trial and error.*

On the board or on chart paper, write the following list:

1. I don't understand the subject at all. I don't even like to go to class.
2. I have some trouble with the subject, but I think it's interesting and I enjoy the class.
3. I can get good grades in the subject, but it really doesn't interest me.
4. I do very well in the subject and I enjoy it, too.

Ask the students to list, on paper, each of their subjects and to write the number of the sentence that best describes how they feel about each class.

When they have finished pass out the sheet "Leadership Styles" to each student. Have them read each style and think about how this information can help them with each of their subjects.

Next, have the students form groups of three or four and share what they have written. Encourage them to discuss how appropriate leadership can help them improve in school and, in particular, how to get the leadership they need.

Discussion Questions:

To facilitate a class discussion ask these and other questions to help the students evaluate what they have learned:

— *How do you feel when you provide leadership?*
— *What does it take to be a leader?*
— *If more people assumed leadership more often, how would we all benefit?*
— *If you know how to do something but are not motivated to do it, what kind of leadership is most likely to help?*
— *How do you feel when someone tries to give you directions for something you already know how to do?*
— *How do you feel when a teacher delegates an assignment (gives almost no directions at all) if you have no idea what to do? How can you ask for the leadership you need in such a situation?*
— *When does it help to have someone sit down and actually work with you to solve a problem or complete an assignment?*
— *How will this information help you ask for the leadership you need in your classes?*

Leadership Styles

For each number you selected, read the corresponding paragraph to find out what kind of leadership you need.

1. You need lots of help and supervision. Ask your teacher, a parent, a tutor, or another student for step-by-step directions on each assignment. Have your work checked frequently. You benefit most from a teacher who is a **"director."** One who lets you know exactly what is expected of you and coaches you through each assignment. You do not have to feel lost and confused. Don't accept these feelings. Ask for the help you need. Don't worry about liking the class. As soon as you know what you're doing, you'll begin to enjoy it.

2. You need direction and supervision as you continue to gain skill in the class. Whenever you don't understand a problem or assignment, ask for clarification. You benefit most from a teacher who is a **"motivator."** One who sees that you are catching on, gives you lots of positive reinforcement, and inspires you to try even harder. The other thing that will help you is to get involved in the class. You know enough to ask lots of questions and contribute to discussions. Do it. This will reinforce your enjoyment of the class and help you pick up the missing skills faster.

3. You are bored with either the subject or the class or both. If you don't need the class, consider substituting one that you like. If the class is required, take responsibility for increasing your levels of participation and enjoyment. Volunteer for an extra-credit assignment that challenges you. Get involved in class discussions. Volunteer for group assignments. You benefit most from a teacher who is a **"participator."** One who invites lots of class participation and interaction. If that's not your teacher's style, see if you can transfer to another teacher.

4. You are so successful and self-motivated in this class that you don't need much leadership at all. You will do the work whether the teacher is there or not. You benefit most from a teacher who is a **"delegator."** One who trusts you enough to say, "Here's the assignment—see what you can do with it." This class offers *you* a chance to be a leader. Be creative. Break new ground. Offer to help students who are having trouble with the class. If you see ways that the class could be improved for everyone, discuss them privately with the teacher.

The teacher is your leader.

Ask for what you need!

Things I Find Useful

(Personal notes and ideas that make this activity work better for me)

The Things I like Best About My Family

Objectives:

The students will:

— focus on the family as a potential source of strength and support.
— understand that families are cooperative organizations that offer security and strength to individuals.

Materials:

writing or drawing materials

Directions:

Begin the session by asking the students to consider the things they like about their families. Elaborate by saying, in your own words:

Sometimes we have difficulty thinking of positive things we value in our own family. However, when we examine our feelings and thoughts closely, we can usually find many positive features, activities, traditions, and traits to talk about. For example, you might especially like the way in which your family communicates. Perhaps you have a very warm, supportive family, or maybe your family is unique because of its language or culture.

Model the kind of contribution you desire, by offering one or two examples from your own family.

Have the students take out writing materials. Ask them to write down all of the positive things they can think of about their family. (If you prefer, have the students draw a picture of a positive quality or feature of their family.)

Allow about 10 minutes for writing (or drawing). When the students have finished, have them form dyads and take turns sharing what they have written (or drawn). Allow about 2 minutes per partner, monitor the process, and call time after each 2-minute interval.

Facilitate a culminating discussion. Ask the questions provided, or develop questions based on your observations during the activity.

Discussion Questions:

1. What similarities and/or differences did you notice in the things you shared with your partner?
2. Why are families so significant in our lives?
3. When you think about your family in this way, do you get any ideas about how you might be able to go to them for help and support? Tell us your ideas.

Things I Find Useful

(Personal notes and ideas that make this activity work better for me)

Tape Recorder Dyad

Objective:

The students will demonstrate attentive listening for content.

Materials:

chalkboard, chalk, and timer or watch

Directions:

1. Briefly explain to the students that listening is an integral part of the communication process. One way to facilitate communication is simply to be silent, giving the person who is speaking a green light to speak without interruptions. The listener further facilitates communication by mentally recording the content of the speaker's monolog.

2. Divide the students into dyads. Attempt to pair students who do not know each other very well. Ask them to determine who will be **A** and who will be **B**.

3. Play two rounds of the activity, as follows:

   First half of round 1:

   Recording:

   A speaks uninterrupted for two minutes to his or her partner about a topic such as : "The Best Thing That's Happened to Me So Far Today." B listens attentively, mentally recording the speaker's data.

   Playback:

   After the speaker's two-minute monolog, the listener is given one-and-a-half minutes to verbally "play back" the data given by the speaker during the "recording session."

   Corrections or additions:

   At the end of the playback, the speaker is given one-half minute to clarify any information the listener didn't understand or to add things the listener forgot.

Second half of round 1:

Reverse roles (**B** speaks, **A** listens) and repeat the entire process (same topic).

First half of round 2:

Person **A** becomes the speaker again. The procedure is exactly the same as for the first half of round 1. However, the topic is changed. A suggestion for the second topic is, "Things I'm Looking Forward to This Semester."

Second half of round 2: Reverse roles (**B** speaks, **A** listens) and repeat the entire process (same topic).

4. **Suggested Topics:**

One of My Favorite Possessions

A Secret Wish I Have

A Person I'd Like To Be Like

My Idea of a Perfect Saturday Afternoon

Someone I Trust

Something I Don't Like Doing

Discussion Questions:

After both rounds have been completed, facilitate a discussion by asking these and other questions. Record key responses on the chalkboard for a quick review:

— *How did you feel as the speaker?*
— *How did you feel as the listener?*
— *Did it get easier or harder in round 2 to function like a tape recorder?*
— *Did you learn anything new and interesting about your partner?*
— *How does silent attentive listening promote effective communication?*
— *How can attentive listening help you succeed in school?*
— *What are some things you can do to show someone you are really listening?*

Things I Find Useful

(Personal notes and ideas that make this activity work better for me)

Steps for Solving a Problem Responsibly

Objective:

The students will develop and practice a process for effective problem-solving.

Materials:

one copy of pages 68 and 69, "Steps for Solving a Problem Responsibly," for each student

Directions:

Distribute the copies of, "Steps for Solving a Problem Responsibly." Ask the students to read each step in the problem-solving process with you and to write notes on their sheet. Generate discussion *after each step* by asking appropriate open-ended questions. Introduce a personal example (a problem that you need to solve) and take it through the process as part of the discussion. If time permits, go back through the process a second time, using as an example a problem described by one of the students.

Discussion Questions:

1. Stop all blaming.

— *What happens when you get bogged down in the blaming game?*
— *What are people who constantly blame others for their problems trying to avoid?*
— *How is blaming others the same as giving away your power?*

2. Define the problem.

— *Why is it so important to know exactly what the problem is?*
— *Why does it matter whether it's your problem or someone else's?*
— *When should people <u>not</u> be left to solve their own problems?*
— *What can happen when a person gets all worked up about a problem that isn't even their's?*

3. Consider asking for help.

— *When is it wise to ask for help?*
— *Who gets to decide what kind of help you need?*
— *If what you want is information or advice, and instead the person tries to solve the problem for you, what can you do?*

4. Think of alternative solutions.

— *What is the advantage of thinking of alternatives?*
— *If you can't think of more than one or two alternatives, what should you definitely do before making a decision?*
— *How does collecting information expand your alternatives?*

5. Evaluate the alternatives.

— *What are some ways of collecting information?*
— *Why not just do the first thing that comes to mind?*
— *Why is it important to imagine what will happen as a result of trying each alternative?*

6. Make a decision.

— *If you still can't make a decision, which steps could you return to? (2., 4., and 5., and 3., in that order. The problem may be incorrectly defined; you may need to gather additional information; the consequences may need further consideration; or help may be called for.)*

7. Follow through.

— *Why stick to a decision?*
— *What can you do if the solution doesn't work or more problems come up?*
— *How can you evaluate your decision?*
— *What's an example of a big problem in our society that used to be a much smaller problem with a relatively easy solution?*

Steps for Solving a Problem Responsibly

1. Stop all blaming.

It will help me to understand that blaming someone (including myself) for the problem will not solve it. If I really want to solve the problem, I need to put my energy into working out a solution. Blaming myself and others is a waste of time.

2. Define the problem

Next, I need to ask myself two questions to help me get started. "What exactly is the problem?" and "Whose problem is it?" If I find that it's not my problem, the best thing I can do is let the people who "own" the problem solve it themselves. Or I can ask them, "How can I help you?"

3. Consider asking for help.

Once I'm sure I "own" the problem and know what it is, I may choose to ask someone for help. For example, I may decide to talk over the problem with someone.

4. Think of alternative solutions.

I need to ask myself: "What are some things I could do about this?" I need to think of <u>as many reasonable ideas for solving the problem as I can</u>. To do this, I will probably need to collect some information.

5. Evaluate the alternatives.

Next, for each idea I come up with I need to ask myself: "What will happen to me and the other people involved if I try this one?" I need to be very honest with myself. If I don't know how someone else will be affected, I need to ask that person, "How will you feel about it if I. . ."

6. Make a decision.

I need to choose the alternative that appears to have the best chance of succeeding. If my solution is a responsible one, it will not hurt anyone unnecessarily—and it will probably work.

7. Follow through.

After I've made the decision, I'll stick to it for a reasonable length of time. If the decision doesn't work, I'll try another alternative. If the decision works, but causes more problems in the process, I'll start all over again to solve them. *And I'll try not to blame myself or anybody else for those problems.*

Things I Find Useful

(Personal notes and ideas that make this activity work better for me)

Decisions and Outcomes

Objectives:

The students will:

— understand and describe how decisions are influenced.
— state the outcomes and possible consequences of specific decisions.
— develop and practice a process for effective decision making.

Materials:

writing materials for each student

Directions:

Begin by defining decision making as a process in which a person selects from two or more choices. Point out that:

- a decision is not necessary unless there is more than one course of action to consider.
- not deciding is making a decision.
- Two people facing similar decisions create unique outcomes because they want different things.
- Learning decision-making skills increases the possibility that a person can have what s/he wants.
- Each decision is limited by what a person is able to do and what s/he is willing to do. Ability is increased by having more alternatives. Willingness is usually determined by values and goals.

Give the students 1 minute to write down all the decisions they can remember making so far today. Give them a little jump start by suggesting decisions like: what to wear, what to eat, when to eat and with whom, whether to go to class, whether to tell the truth, what to say to someone, etc.

On the chalkboard draw a scale from 0 to 5, as follows:

0 = no control, decision made by others

1 = automatic, routine, habitual

2 = occasionally think about it

3 = think about, but don't study it

4 = study a little bit

5 = study a lot

Ask the students to go back through their list of decisions and code each one with a number from the scale. Give them a minute or two to do this and then ask for a show of hands relative to numbers of decisions in each category of the scale.

Next, ask the students to think of the worst decision they ever made and write a brief description of it on paper. Give them several minutes to accomplish this. Then ask the students to share what they have written with a partner. (Make it clear that sharing is voluntary. Some students may not wish to divulge their worst decision.)

Writing important points on the chalkboard, make the following observations about decisions and outcomes:

- When most people say a decision is poor, they mean the <u>result is not what they wanted</u>.
- Good decision making minimizes the possibility of getting bad outcomes, but it doesn't eliminate the possibility.
- A decision is the act of choosing among several possibilities based on your judgments.
- An outcome is the result, consequence, or aftermath of the decision.
- A person has direct control over the decision, but not over the outcome.
- A good decision does not guarantee a good outcome, but it does *increase* the chances of a good outcome.

Discussion Questions:

Ask the students to get back together with their partner and reevaluate their "worst decision." Then facilitate a total class discussion by asking these and other questions:

— *What did you find out about your "worst decision" from this activity?*
— *What is the difference between decisions and outcomes?*
— *If your decision was truly bad, how could you have made a better one?*
— *What kinds of decisions require study and thought?*
— *How can having decision-making skills help you in school? ...in your job? ...after high school?*

Things I Find Useful

(Personal notes and ideas that make this activity work better for me)

Decisions, Decisions!

Objectives:

The students will:

— understand and describe how decisions are influenced.
— develop and practice a process for effective decision making.

Materials:

writing materials for each student

Directions:

On the chalkboard or chart paper, copy the "Decision-Making Process" listed on page 78, Read through the decision-making steps with the students, examining each one. Here are some ideas to discuss and questions to ask:

• Knowing what is important to you and what you want to accomplish involves such things as likes/dislikes, values, and interests. Most important, it involves having goals. As the Cheshire Cat said to Alice: "If you don't know where you're going, any road will take you there."

• You can get information by talking to people, visiting places, watching TV, and reading. Once you have the information, you must be able to evaluate it. If two people tell you to do opposite things, how are you going to know which is right? What if neither is right?

• Look into the future. Ask yourself what would be the probable outcome if you chose each of the alternatives available. For example, what would happen if:

— you did not go to college?
— you never got married?
— you dropped out of school?
— you decided to experiment with drugs?
— you became a professional rock singer?
— you decided never to drink alcohol?
— you decided not to have children?
— How did you make your predictions? What information did you use?

- When you reach the decision point, don't procrastinate. If you've done a good job on the other steps, you can choose the best alternative with confidence. Remember, if you don't choose, someone else may choose for you.

- Not every decision requires an action plan, but the big ones usually do. The decision to attend a 4-year college in another state won't come true unless you make it. And that means more decisions. Can you think what they are?

Next, ask the students to go through the process for themselves. On a sheet of paper, have them respond as you ask the following questions:

1. Think of a decision that you need to make in the next month. Define (describe) the decision on your paper.

2. What kinds of things that are important in your life (your values) might affect or be affected by this decision?

3. What kinds of information do you have or need?

   a. things to think about
   b. people to talk to
   c. things to read
   d. things to do

4. List your alternatives.

5. List the advantages and disadvantages at each alternative.

6. Now make a decision! Which alternative has the best chance of producing the outcome you want?

7. Last, write a plan for putting this decision into action. List the steps of your plan in order of their occurrence.

When the students have completed their decision-making process, ask them to choose partners and take turns sharing their decisions and decision-making process.

Discussion Questions:

Facilitate a class discussion. Ask these and other questions:

— *What did you learn about decision-making from this activity?*
— *What can happen if you put off making a decision?*
— *Why is it important to know your interests and values when making decisions?*
— *How can having goals help you make decisions?*

The Decision-Making Process

Here are some steps to follow when you have a decision to make:

1. Recognize and define the decision to be made.

2. Know what is important to you — your values — and what you want to accomplish — your goal.

3. Study the information you have already; obtain and study new information, too.

4. List all of your alternatives.

5. List the advantages and disadvantages of each alternative.

6. Make a decision.

7. Develop a plan for carrying out your decision.

Things I Find Useful

(Personal notes and ideas that make this activity work better for me)

We Can Have Enjoyable Careers!

Objectives:

The students will:

— recognize that many possible jobs relate to the things they enjoy doing.

— identify and describe things that they can do to prepare for a career.

Materials:

A chart displaying this list of career areas: *Business, Materials Science; Transportation; Agricultural Technology; Health; Public Service; Sports and Recreation; Environmental Control; Manufacturing; Communications; Music; Art.* Chart paper and magic marker.

Directions:

Ask the students to look with you at the list of career areas. Talk about the careers people have in each area. Here are some examples: Business: word processor; Materials Science: quality assurance; Transportation: airline pilot; Agricultural Technology: farmer; Health: medical doctor; Public Service: policeman/policewoman; Sports and Recreation: baseball coach; Environmental Control: city planner; Manufacturing: robotic engineer; Communications: newspaper reporter; Music: guitarist; Art: graphic designer.

Ask the students to list five things they really like to do. Tell them these should be fun things that interest them a lot. Explain to the students that a few people decide when they are children or teens exactly what career they want, prepare for it, and go directly into it when they become adults. However, most people change their minds many times. And most adults change careers several times. So while it's not necessary for them to choose a career now, it is helpful to talk about the possibilities.

Have the students brainstorm all of the possible jobs they can think of that relate to their recorded "likes." Ask volunteers to read to the group one thing from their list that they like to do, and do well. After the first person has read from his/her list, have the group brainstorm jobs that relate to that person's interest area. Record ideas on chart paper.

Continue in this manner until jobs have been brainstormed for at least one item from each student's list.

Discussion Questions:

Ask the students:

— *How can you best prepare for a future in which you will change careers several times?*
— *What are some things you are doing now that you could earn money doing as an adult?*

Things I Find Useful

(Personal notes and ideas that make this activity work better for me)

How Networks Work

Objectives:

The students will:

— understand the concept of networking as it applies to achieving a goal

— describe how networking facilitates job seeking.

Materials:

a chart duplicating the diagram shown on page 85.

Directions:

Ask the students if they have ever heard the word *network*, and talk with them about its meaning.

Show the students the chart and tell them: *Here's how a network works: The people in Rows 1 and 4 have wants and needs. But they don't even know each other. The people in Row 1 only know the people in Row 2. The people in Row 2 only know the people in Rows 1 and 3. The people in Row 3 only know the people in Rows 2 and 4. The people in Row 4 only know the people in Row 3. So, in order for the people in Rows 1 and 4 to find each other, they have to get help from the people in Rows 2 and 3.*

Tell this story about the first person in Row 1: *Joe wants a puppy so he puts the word out to a lot of people. One person he tells is Rick, and Rick says, "My cousin, Sallie, has a friend whose dog had puppies about two months ago." Joe asks Rick for Sallie's phone number and calls her up. He says hello and explains that her cousin, Rick, is one of his friends. He tells her he is looking for a new puppy, and that Rick said she has a friend whose dog had puppies. Sallie responds, "Yes. Her name is Shirley and she lives about a block from me." Joe gets Shirley's phone number from Sallie. Then he calls Shirley and asks if he can see the puppies. When he sees the puppies, he chooses one and takes it home.*

Everybody is happy.

Pick five volunteers to act out the story, playing the roles of the four children and one pup.

After the drama, applaud the actors. Then have new volunteers plan and act out the other three networks shown on the chart.

Discussion Questions:

After all of the dramas have been acted out, ask the students:

— *What does this activity teach us about how friends can help us get what we want?*
— *What are some things we should say when we contact people we don't know?*
— *How can you use networking to help you get a job?*
— *Do you have any ideas about how networking might help you in any area of school?*

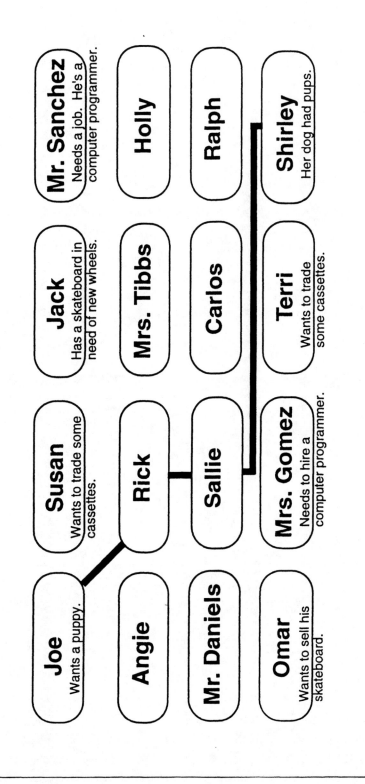

85

Things I Find Useful

(Personal notes and ideas that make this activity work better for me)

I Made a Plan and It Worked

Objectives:

The students will:

— describe the importance of planning to goal attainment.
— identify steps in the planning process.

Directions:

Begin this session by explaining to the students that today you want to focus on goal setting, and how important planning is if you want to reach a goal.

Ask the students to form dyads so that each student can speak for 2 minutes to the topic "I Made a Plan and It Worked." Elaborate on the topic by saying something like: *Think of a time when you had a task or project to complete and, rather than leave it to chance, to someone else, or to a last minute rush job, you planned it out. Maybe you made a list of objectives—things that had to be done to complete the task. Or perhaps you made a "to-do" list, and checked each item off as you did it. The project could have been in connection with a class assignment, a club fund raiser, a school election, a party, or just about anything. What matters here is that you thought about it, and you developed a plan to make things turn out the way you wanted them to. Think it over for a minute. The topic is, "I Made a Plan, and It Worked."*

Discussion Questions:

Call time after 2 minutes and have the students switch roles. After all students had their 2 minutes to speak, encourage a discussion by asking these and other questions:

— *What's the most important thing you have to know in order to make a plan? (your goal)*
— *What happens if you try to accomplish a complicated task without any kind of plan?*
— *What is it like to work with other people on a project without a plan?*
— *How do the questions* What? How? When? *and* Who? *relate to planning?*
— *How do you feel when you plan something and your plan works?*

Things I Find Useful

(Personal notes and ideas that make this activity work better for me)

You Gotta Have Goals!

Objectives:

The students will:

— identify personal goals in a number of areas
— develop a written action plan for one goal

Materials:

writing materials for each student

Directions:

Begin by defining what goals are. For example: *A goal is an end, home base, the final destination, what you are aiming for. Goals can center on having something—clothes, a car, money—or they can center on achieving—finishing school, going to college, having a career, becoming famous, gaining knowledge and honors.*

Next, discuss with the students the difference between short-term and long-range goals:

Short-term goals include making phone calls, finishing your homework, cleaning your room, doing your chores, or making plans for the weekend. Long-range goals might include planning a trip for next summer; deciding to go to a trade school, a community college, or a university; saving money to buy something special; or making some plans for your future career.

Have each student prepare a sheet of paper like the sample at the end of this activity.

When the students have prepared their sheets, have them:

1. write one goal in each area,
2. check whether it is a short-term or long-range goal, and
3. write the date by which they hope to accomplish the goal.

When everyone has completed this part of the activity, ask the students to select one goal to work on further. Have them turn their papers over, and write that goal at the top of the page.

Direct the students to think of any roadblocks that might interfere with reaching the goal, and write those down, too. Next, have the students list strategies for overcoming each roadblock. Walk around and offer assistance and clarification, as necessary.

Finally, have the students describe in writing other steps that they must take to reach their goal, and write down a completion date for each step. Again, circulate among the students and offer help where needed.

Conclude this experience by asking the students to form dyads and share the goal they have been working on, along with the roadblocks, strategies for overcoming the roadblocks, and positive steps for reaching their goal. Make sure each student has the chance to fully discuss his or her goal and the steps to achieving it.

My Goals

	Goals	Short Term	Long Range	Completion Date
School				
Career				
Family				
Personal				
Social				

Things I Find Useful

(Personal notes and ideas that make this activity work better for me)

Improving the Study Habit

Objectives;

The students will:

— learn and practice effective study habits.
— develop and implement plans for self-improvement.

Directions:

Begin by asking students where and how they study. Call on volunteers to to share their study strategies. List particularly helpful or innovative ideas on the chalkboard. Tell the students that you are going to share some additional study tips with them. Explain that, if they are willing to incorporate these suggestions two or three at a time, they will soon be more successful students. Have the students take notes in their journals or notebooks as you present the following ideas (You may want to list the tips that are in bold on chart paper or a chalk board to make it easier for the students to understand each point):

1. **Plan a specific time to study for each class.** Most students making the transition from elementary to middle/junior high or from middle/junior high to high school fail to recognize that more is expected of them. Most teachers assign homework on a daily basis.

2. **Study the difficult subjects first.** The difficult classes demand more energy than the easier ones, so save the "light" subjects for later.

3. **Schedule short, frequent breaks during study or home-work sessions.** Whenever possible, study for approximately 20 minutes and take a 5-minute break; then study again for about 20 minutes and take another 5-minute break. We tend to remember better what we learn at the beginning and end of each study period, so create more beginnings and end-ings. Give your brain a break.

4. **Study at your best time of the day.** Some of us are morning people and function most effectively during the early morning hours. Others of us are most productive in the afternoon or evening. Study your most difficult subjects during your optimum time period.

5. **Establish a special study area.** Select a place that you can use only for study. This should not be on your bed or near a television. Your body and mind are trained to respond to their environment. Your body has learned that a bed is a place for rest; your mind knows that the television is a tool for relaxation and entertainment. Study at a desk or table. Give your body the signal that it is time to study, not time to sleep.

6. **Study in a quiet place.** Don't study in front of a television or near a loud stereo. The majority of research clearly shows that the optimum way to study is in silence or with soft music with a slow beat—not to the accompaniment of TV or loud, fast-beat music.

7. **Avoid using the phone during scheduled study time.** If someone else can answer the phone, have that person take messages. Then, return your calls later. If you are the only one home, let an answering machine take the message. If you *must* answer the phone, do so with the clear intention of taking a brief message and/or calling back after you have finished studying.

8. **Make good use of the scheduled study time.** If you haven't accomplished what you planned, review your actions and notice the ways in which you wasted time. Since we are creatures of habit, we tend to waste time in the same ways again and again.

9. **Pretend you are a "paid" student.** If you were employed as a student, would you be earning your wages? If your breaks were longer than your study sessions, you would probably have your pay "docked," or lose your job.

10. **Push yourself to finish an assignment.** Sometimes we let ourselves get close, but decide that we are too tired or busy to finish an assignment. If you can press yourself to finish, you will establish a habit of accomplishing what you set out to do.

Ask the students to respond in writing to the following directions:

1. Brainstorm for five minutes, listing the different ways you waste time.

2. Review the list. Choose two time-wasters that you use often and write a note to yourself (as if you were someone else) about why these time wasters are so attractive to you. Ask yourself what you are getting out of using them, and what they are costing you, too. Write down your answers.

3. Review the list again and select three time wasters that you are willing to reduce or eliminate.

Discussion Questions:

Lead a culminating discussion. Ask these and other questions:

— *What are some of your biggest time wasters?*
— *Which ones are the most difficult to give up?*
— *How can you improve your study habits?*
— *Which study tips do you plan to try?*
— *Whom do you need to ask for help or support in order to carry out your improved study plan?*

Things I Find Useful

(Personal notes and ideas that make this activity work better for me)

Time Management Inventory

Objectives:

The students will:

— develop an awareness of how they spend their time.
— identify time wasters that hinder their ability to accomplish goals.

Materials:

writing materials for each student

Directions:

Direct the students to create a Time Management Inventory sheet by listing the time they get up at the top left of the sheet and then continuing to list the time in half-hour increments (until they go to bed) down the left side of the paper. Ask the students to record their activities over a three-day period. Suggest that they carry a sheet with them throughout the day, and fill it in as they go. They may think that they will be able to recall their activities at the end of the day, but will likely find this a difficult if not impossible task.

Ask the students to code each activity to show the degree of satisfaction they experienced. A (+) means the student is satisfied that the time was spent productively. A (0) means the student is not satisfied but feels the activity was necessary and required some amount of time. A (-) means the student is dissatisfied and believes the activity was unnecessary.

After three days, have the students total the amount of time spent in categories such as socializing; family activities; in-class time, homework, phone calls; commuting; shopping; errands; employment; eating; household chores; quiet recreation, such as watching television, reading, and listening to music; and active recreation, such as playing tennis, bicycling, and dancing.

Ask the students to judge whether or not they are satisfied with the amount of time spent on each major category of activities. The next time you meet with the students discuss what they learned about how they spent their time and what they can do in the future to use their time more productively.

Things I Find Useful

(Personal notes and ideas that make this activity work better for me)

Daily TO-DO Lists

Objectives:

The students will:

— develop an awareness of the value of a TO-DO list
— write a personal TO-DO list

Materials:

writing materials or a copy of the TO-DO list on page 100 for each student

Directions:

Begin this session by discussing with the students the value of using a TO-DO list. Cover such benefits as:

Students who regularly make TO-DO lists have a much greater chance of accomplishing their goals. Trying to remember appointments, homework assignments, meetings, and other tasks robs students of energy and attention more properly devoted to the business at hand, whether that be listening, computing, reading, studying, or relating. Once a TO-DO list is written, students no longer have to worry about remembering— they merely have to train themselves to refer to the list several times a day. Making TO-DO lists also allows students to prioritize their activities so that the most important tasks are handled first.

Help the students to develop their own TO-DO list. Use the list on page 100 as a model (or copy the list and distribute one to each student). Guide the students through the process of filling out the first sheet in class. Fill out one yourself, as a model. Directions for filling out the TO-DO list:

- Remind the students of their short-term and long-range goals. If they have done planning around each of their goals, they will know what tasks they must accomplish before the goal can be realized. Have the students list the most immediate of these tasks on their first "TO-DO List," along with appointments, meetings, chores, homework assignments, etc.

- Discuss the prioritization process and show the students how you would prioritize the tasks on your own "TO-DO List," using the **A, B, C** method.

In the TO-DO column, list tasks you want to complete today. If the task *must* be completed, check the **A** column; if it would be *nice* to complete it today, check the **B** column, and if it can *wait* without creating a problem, check the **C** column. Write down your estimate of how long each task will take. Prioritize your **A** tasks. Complete your most important **A** task first, and move through the list completing the remainder of the **A** tasks. Then, prioritize the **B** tasks and complete as many as you have time for. When you have finished the task, check the "Completed" column.

Urge the students to keep their list with them throughout the following day, checking off each task as it is completed. Point out that the questions at the bottom of the sheet are intended to help them review their accomplishments at the end of the day.

As soon as possible after the target day on which they use their "TO-DO List," give the students an opportunity to discuss the experience. Reinforce them for accomplishing the tasks they set out to do, and encourage them to use positive self-talk to reinforce and reward themselves.

To - Do List

A	B	C	To-Do Tasks	Time Estimate	Completed (✓)

Things I Find Useful

(Personal notes and ideas that make this activity work better for me)

Study Buddies

Objectives:

The students will:

— discuss and demonstrate the benefits of cooperative learning.
— learn and practice effective study habits.

Directions:

Begin this activity by observing that education often seems more like competition than cooperation as students compete for good grades. Yet everyone's job is easier when teacher and students pull together to try to ensure that school is a "win-win" situation—one in which all students succeed. Point out that people are social and generally enjoy and draw power from working in groups. Ask the students to help you brainstorm some of the benefits of working cooperatively. Quickly list their comments on the chalkboard. Be sure to include these items:

- camaraderie and fun

- support and encouragement

- extra brainpower

- incentive to stick to scheduled study times

- strength and energy when you're tired or discouraged

- a chance to build rewarding relationships

Ask the students to take notes while you offer these guidelines for studying in groups:

1. Studying with friends is okay if joking around, playing music, etc., does not interfere with the real purpose of getting together, which is to study.

2. Study groups should be limited to four or five people.

3. If possible, rotate the location of study groups from home to home. Study outdoors occasionally if the weather permits. If possible, have the host student provide soft drinks, lemonade, or juice.

4. At the end of each meeting, clarify the location of the next meeting, the subject to be studied, and the materials needed. Hold each member responsible for arriving with appropriate materials, ready to contribute to a productive session.

Offer these suggestions for things to do in the study groups:

1. **Test each other by asking questions about material from lectures, reading assignments, and notes.** For example, have each group member write four or five test questions to bring to each study session. Compile the questions and have everyone take the test as a way of reviewing and identifying areas where study is needed.

2. **Practice teaching each other the material.** One of the best ways to learn something is to teach it. Divide up the material and have members take turns instructing the rest of the group on the main points related to their portion.

3. **Compare and contrast notes.** Have everyone contribute his/her notes from lectures or reading assignments or both. Compare the notes and use this as a gauge in deciding which material is most important—if everyone wrote it down, consider it significant. Ask questions about anything that is confusing.

4. **Brainstorm test questions as a group.** After teaching each other and comparing notes, as a group spend 5 to 10 minutes brainstorming possible test questions. Compile a list (along with those questions created individually) in a special section of your notebook.

Announce that you are going to conduct an experiment in group study by having the students prepare for a test in groups.

Arbitrarily divide the class into groups of four or five. Working individually, have the students each develop four test questions related to a recent class assignment. Tell them to take turns asking their group the questions as a kind of pretest to determine where the group needs to concentrate its study efforts.

Then have the group divide up the information to be learned and assign each individual a section to teach the group at the following meeting. End the second session with a 5- to 10-minute brainstorm of test questions covering the entire assignment.

Test the class on the assigned material and grade the tests in your usual manner.

Discussion Questions:

Lead a culminating discussion. Ask the students these and other questions to help them debrief the experience:

— *How did you do on the test?*
— *How does studying with a group compare to studying alone?*
— *What is the most difficult part of studying with a group? What is the easiest part? ...the best part?*
— *What else have you learned about the dynamics of studying with a group?*

Things I Find Useful

(Personal notes and ideas that make this activity work better for me)

Encouraging Ourselves

Objectives:

The students will:

- recognize and describe their own worth and worthiness.
- define themselves physically, emotionally, socially, and intellectually.
- identify strengths, talents, and special abilities in themselves and others.
- practice methods of positive self-talk.

Materials:

stop watch, timer, or watch with a second hand

Directions:

Begin by discussing the fact that each student is an expert on him or herself. No one knows more about the values, hopes, dreams, feelings, and achievements of an individual than the individual. Explain that the students are going to have an opportunity in this activity to clarify important things about their achievements and aspirations.

Ask the students to form dyads (groups of two). Explain that you are going to announce a topic and that the members of each dyad will take turns speaking to the topic for two minutes each. While one partner is speaking, the other will listen carefully; at the end of two minutes, they will switch roles. You will be the timekeeper. After both partners have finished speaking to the topic, everyone will find a new partner and the process will be repeated with a different topic.

Begin the first round. Call time at the end of 2 minutes. Call time again after 2 more minutes and tell the students to find new partners.

Announce a new topic and repeat the procedure.

SUGGESTED TOPICS:

> "Something I Did or Made That I'm Proud Of"
> "Something I Do Well That I Could Earn Money Doing in the Future"
> "My Favorite Hobby or Activity"
> "My Favorite Subject or Class"
> "Something I Enjoy Doing Because It Gives Me a Feeling of Accomplishment"
> "My Favorite Fantasy About What I Could Do with My Life"
> "Something I'm Really Good at That I Haven't Told People About"
> "A Class in Which I'm Improving"

A few minutes before the end of the period, ask the students to pair up again with their first dyad partner. Tell the students to take turns briefly describing the most important things they learned about 1) themselves, and 2) one of their partners during the activity.

Discussion Questions:

Lead a culminating discussion. Ask these and other open-ended questions:

— *Why is it important to talk about our achievements?*
— *What makes a class or project important to you?*
— *What can you do to make more classes interesting to you?*
— *Who is responsible for whether or not you achieve in school?*

Things I Find Useful

(Personal notes and ideas that make this activity work better for me)

Affirmations

Objectives:

The students will:

— identify areas of personal strength.
— develop a series of personal affirmations.

Materials:

writing materials and/or journals or notebooks for each student

Directions:

By deliberately affirming that they do certain things well, students reinforce their strengths and positive attributes. Knowing that students are inclined to focus on their weaknesses, you can go a step further and show students how to construct positive affirmations around skills, abilities, and qualities they would like to cultivate or improve.

Ask the students to take out their journals or notebooks, and to list ten things that they do well. Tell them to include anything that they feel good about, small or large, such as reading, dancing, pitching a fast ball, running, working on a computer, being a friend, etc.

While the students are preparing their list on the chalkboard, write these guidelines for constructing an affirmation:

- Write the affirmation in the present tense. Say "I am..." rather than "I will... ."

- Be specific. For example, if gymnastics is your focus, specify in which areas of gymnastics you are improving, such as parallel bars, rings, free style, etc.

- Repeat each affirmation often. Picture yourself exhibiting the attribute or performing the skill perfectly.

Circulate throughout the class and offer suggestions and positive descriptions of skills, where necessary. When all lists have been completed, ask the students to choose three items from their list, and to write an affirmation for each one. Read and discuss the guidelines that are written on the board. Provide some examples such as, "I enjoy reading," "I'm a terrific dancer," or "I'm a good friend." Next have the students list five things they would like to do <u>better</u>. Provide some examples, such as improving math skills, public speaking, making new friends, or playing a musical instrument. When this list is complete ask the students to choose two items from this list and to write an affirmation for each one. Remind them to write it as if they <u>already have</u> the skill or ability. Provide examples such as, "Math comes easily to me," "I am poised and confident when speaking to a group," or "I make new friend every week."

Have the students get together in dyads or triads and practice delivering their affirmations aloud and with conviction. Urge the students to coach and encourage each other.

Things I Find Useful

(Personal notes and ideas that make this activity work better for me)

Success Bombardment

Objectives:

The students will:

- recognize and describe their own worth and worthiness.
- define themselves physically, emotionally, socially, and intellectually.
- identify strengths, talents, and special abilities in themselves and others.
- practice methods of positive self-talk.

Materials:

journals or notebooks and 12 small self-adhesive labels per student

Directions:

Begin this session by asking the students to think of successes they have had. Remind them that their life is really a series of successes, one after another, year after year. Tell the students that you would like them to look back and recall some of the many things they have learned and achieved. In their journals or notebooks, have the students list five skills they mastered before the age of 5. When this list is complete, ask them to list four things they accomplish between 5 and 8. Next, four achievements between 8 and 11. Then, three major accomplishments between 11 and 13 and, finally, three successes between 13 and the present (modify these instructions to suit the age range of the group). Have the students work individually to complete their lists. Allow about 15 minutes. If the students appear to be having trouble thinking of accomplishments, take a couple of minutes and talk with the entire class about such examples as leaning to: *walk, talk, dress, dance, play, sing, count, problem-solve, read, write, love; ride a bike, skateboard, roller-skate; ski, play softball, volleyball, soccer, basketball; cook, play an instrument, use a computer, be a friend, join an organization; earn a merit badge, award, or certificate; learn to type, baby-sit, drive a car, care for a pet; etc., etc.*

When the students have completed their lists, ask them to form groups of four or five. Give 12 small, blank, self-adhesive labels to each student.

Direct the students to take turns describing their accomplishments to the other members of their group. In your own words, explain: *Tell your group why you picked those particular successes. Explain how you felt about them at the time they occurred and why they are particularly meaningful to you now. <u>Immediately after you share</u>, the other members of your group will <u>each</u> make three labels that describe positive things about you based on the successes you shared. For example, the first person's labels might say, "industrious and energetic," "musically talented," and "born to lead." Then, that person will look directly at you, tell you what he or she has written on each label, and stick the labels in your journal (notebook). The other members of your group will then take a turn "bombarding" you with their success labels in the same manner. If there are three other people in your group (total of four), you will end up with nine labels in your journal (notebook). A second person in the group will then take a turn reading his or her successes and being "bombarded;" then a third person will be the target, and so on until everyone has had a turn to be "bombarded."*

Circulate and assist the groups, as needed. Although the students are expected to enjoy the exercise, make sure that they appreciate its seriousness and do not engage in any kind of teasing or put-downs. If you observe any student using the third person ("*She* is industrious and energetic.") when labeling a "target," stop the person and help him/her rephrase the statement in the second person ("You are industrious and energetic").

Discussion Questions:

— *How do you feel after doing this exercise?*
— *What did you learn about yourself? ...about other members of your group?*
— *How did you decide which accomplishments to include on your list?*
— *Why do you suppose we spend so much time thinking about our failures and deficiencies when we have all accomplished so much?*
— *What can you do with your list so that it will continue to remind you of your successes?*

Things I Find Useful

(Personal notes and ideas that make this activity work better for me)

Achievement Potential Follow-up Survey Summary Sheet

Using the information provided with your *Achievement Potential Survey* and the insights you've gained about yourself, review each of the 26 achievement factors and place an X in the appropriate Asset, Barrier, or Concern to reflect where you are NOW in your perceptions. Then compare your ratings with your previous Summary Sheet and, in the last column, indicate whether your rating now is in a positive (+) direction (Barrier to Concern, Concern to Asset, etc.), negative (-) direction (Asset to Concern, Concern to Barrier, etc.), or no change (0).

Part I. <u>Can</u> I do well in school?

	Asset	Barrier	Concern	+ ,-;0
1. Academic Ability				
2. Current Knowledge				
3. Past Experiences				
4. Study Skills				
5. Learning Style				
6. Seeing Connections				

Part II. Do I really <u>want</u> to do well in school?

	Asset	Barrier	Concern	+ ,-;0
7. General Mood				
8. Health				
9. Feelings About Achievement				
10. Life/Career Goals				
11. Impressing Others				
12. Risking Failure				
13. Tackling Unpleasant Tasks				
14. Sticking With a Problem				
15. Time Spent on Homework				

Part III. What effect have my family and friends had on my achievement?

	Asset	Barrier	Concern	+ ,-,0
16. Family's Expectations				
17. Family's Support				
18. Friends' Expectations				
19. Friends' Support				

Part IV. How "inviting" is my school?

	Asset	Barrier	Concern	+ ,-,0
20. Difficulty of School Work				
21. Nature of Assignments				
22. Teachers' Expectations				
23. Teachers' Support				
24. School Resources				
25. School Climate				
26. Extracurricular Activities				

About the Authors

Jeanne C. Bleuer, Ph.D., is Associate Director of the ERIC Clearinghouse on Counseling and Student Services at the University of North Carolina at Greensboro. Dr. Bleuer is a nationally recognized researcher and writer on student learning and achievement, and her major interest is translating research into practical concepts and activities which teachers and counselors can use to enhance student achievement. She is the author of *Counseling Underachievers*, the original book in this two volume series.

Susanna Palomares, M.Ed., is president of Innerchoice Publishing in Spring Valley, California. Susanna is a former classroom teacher and is a nationally known trainer in the area of social-emotional development in students. She has authored and co-authored a number of other books for use by teachers and counselors in the social-emotional realm.

Garry R. Walz, Ph.D., is Professor Emeritus from the University of Michigan and Director of the ERIC Clearinghouse on Counseling and Student Services at the University of North Carolina at Greensboro. A past President of the American Counseling Association and the Association for Counselor Education and Supervision, Dr. Walz is a nationally known researcher, writer, and speaker on student learning and self-esteem and critical issues in counselor education.